OLD ROOMS
FOR NEW LIVING

OLD ROOMS
FOR
NEW LIVING

Being a collection of
EARLY AMERICAN INTERIORS
Authentic in design
Various in period
and suitable for
TODAY'S LIVING
This is a
TREASURY OF TRADITION
for the home decorator

by

NARCISSA CHAMBERLAIN

PHOTOGRAPHS BY
SAMUEL CHAMBERLAIN

HASTINGS HOUSE

PUBLISHERS   NEW YORK

CONTENTS

OLD ROOMS FOR NEW LIVING

THESE pictures have been gathered together that you may see in authentic and original form the rooms of the past, their charm and practicality, and the beauty and changing style developed in New England houses from our beginnings. This is a guidebook for the home owner or decorator who wishes to preserve in practical modern surroundings our American inheritance of good taste. The intention has been to make this a source book of ideas for decorating a whole house or the corner of a single room. Perhaps you need a suggestion for placing one fine old piece of your grandmother's. Here are groups and corners, arrangements and details to inspire and help you.

Men do not change, only the conditions in which they live. A fire on the open hearth is just as cherished a symbol of cheer and comfort as it ever was, though bed warmers and kitchen pumps are long departed features of our daily life. What was truly good in design and usefulness in our ancestors' homes remains good today, and there is no reason to reject it because the modern house is a normal development of twentieth century practicality. In fact, what is good from various periods can be happily mingled in decorating a home because basic principles do not change, only their expressions through the ages. A primitive wall cupboard over the fireplace has not lost its charm for the simple reason that a wall cupboard is a useful thing, and fills otherwise wasted space. The adaptability of 18th-century styles to modern living is evident. It is not necessary to cook over the open hearth (though it can be fun too!) nor to read by candlelight, in order to profit by what the past has to offer. However, well designed paneling, original corner cupboards, and four-post beds are as beautiful as they ever were, and the television set is as well housed in a distinguished old cabinet as in its modern counterpart. A taproom bar from an old New England tavern offers a perfect model for use in a present day kitchen-dining room or playroom.

These interiors are not flawless. Where hand-wrought iron thumb-latches have been unfortunately replaced by china door knobs, such a defect is not to be imitated. Nor has a contemporary copy of an old house any need for the exposed heating pipes or incongruous window curtains which may appear in occasional illustrations. But the mingling of styles sometimes depicted here can be happily imitated with a little taste and judgment. Fine contemporary copies of old furniture are obtainable in these days of serious restoration projects, such as those at Williamsburg, Virginia, and Sturbridge, Massachusetts. A fine reproduction of a wing chair is as comfortable today as in the 18th century, and no more difficult to obtain than certain obese, "over-stuffed" specimens which lack the grace of the earlier period.

No attempt has been made to give a complete and scholarly analysis of the history and origins of American domestic styles. Our museums and libraries offer wonderful material for further research to anyone whose interest is stimulated by this simple book. Rather the intention here has been to compile as concisely and as accurately as possible, an outline of

2

this fascinating subject as a guide to decoration. It is illustrated with photographs of original or authentically restored interiors that have added warmth and character from being lived in. These are rooms used by human beings who had the same problems and desires as you and I, the need for comfort combined with beauty which persists through all periods in human history. These pictures are offered, then, as an inspiration to those who would ornament their own homes, with the realization that nothing that is fine in design, and practical in function, is ever really out of date. The present and the future can never be separated from the past from which they have grown and evolved.

Old houses and old furniture acquire tangible personalities of their own through years of association with the living beings who have used them. This sense of character is elusive but priceless. It is something to be conserved and treasured in your surroundings. It is here for anyone with seeing eyes.

AMERICAN STYLES

Periods did not begin nor end abruptly on exact dates, and the natural transition from one style to another gives a sound precedent for considered mingling of styles in the same house. For purposes of convenience the material in this book has been roughly classified into five groups: Early American, Mid-Colonial, Georgian-Colonial, Federal, and Post-Federal (after 1815–1820). However, we choose to ignore the decorative disasters of the last half of the 19th century and close our book somewhat hastily, as well as apologetically, with just a few samples of pre-mid-century American rooms.

EARLY AMERICAN
The Early American Period includes styles from the 17th-century Pilgrim days approximately up to the second quarter of the 18th century. Houses were primitive and Elizabethan in character. Construction, rather than ornamentation, dominated the interior, where beams, posts, rafters,

3

and sometimes the chimney itself were left exposed. This enormous chimney became literally the heart and center of the house, answering all heating and cooking needs. Roofs were steep-pitched gables. Narrow, sometimes enclosed stairs led from a small entry to the upper floor. On one side of this entry was the general kitchen-living-room, following the tradition of the English "hall." Perhaps there was a room at the back against the same chimney, and a larger house may have had still another room at the other side of the entry. The beauty of the early interior is based on functionalism plus naïve simplicity. The very wide fireplace with heavy wood lintel had an oven built into the bricks beside it, and was sometimes covered above and at the sides by simple pine boards known as sheathing. These wide boards were placed edge to edge, or joined by a sort of tongue-and-groove method, and were trimmed by a "shadow" molding at the joint. This consisted of several shallow grooves or lines paralleling the seam. Slightly later a "feathered" molding was used, a method of joining the boards by beveling one side and fitting the narrow edge of the bevel into a slot in the next board.

Small cupboards or shelves were often built in against the sloping brick of the fireplace above the great wood lintel, and at the sides were other cupboards and ovens. Wide pine sheathing was used vertically to form partitions between the rooms, or horizontally (for easier fastening to the uprights) to line the rooms' outer walls. Or these were sometimes covered with rough plaster which was made with a base of clam or oyster shells for lack of limestone. Wallpaper did not appear until the second half of the 18th century. Sometimes the sheathing was joined to ceiling beam and fireplace edge by a simple primitive dentil molding with bits of bright red earth color in the indentations, as well as along the edges of chamfered * beams. In about 1725 when paint and stain began to be used on trim, it was of such colors as a rust or India red, olive green, blue green, and certain deep blues and ochres. White paint did not appear until toward the end of the 18th century.

The first latches were probably of wood, and leather strips took the

* Chamfered—Beveled or flattened off the length of its angular edge.

place of hinges on batten doors. These were made of vertical boards held together by horizontal strips of wood, or battens. Soon hinges, thumb-latches, nails and various fireside and cooking implements were made of hand-wrought iron.

The early small, leaded window of medieval character could not have admitted much light, but had the advantage of conserving some heat during the cold New England winter. It was not long before windows became larger as glass became less of a luxury, and the small-paned, two-sash window with heavy wood muntins, was the style during most of the 18th century.

MID-COLONIAL

The Mid-Colonial Period covers the second quarter and the middle of the 18th century. As men became more prosperous they embellished their houses with simple rectangular beveled paneling, boxed in the exposed beams, and plastered the ceilings. Thus we come into what we have chosen to classify here as the second period of the early American house, or Mid-Colonial. The completely paneled fireplace "end" with balanced cupboard doors, or perhaps corner cupboards, was the featured decoration of a room, the other walls remaining plastered or covered to chair height with a paneled wainscot. There were occasional panels raised beyond the surface of the woodwork, particularly over the fireplace opening. Between 1720 and 1750 simple classic pilasters began to appear, bolection * moldings, and more elaborate cornice moldings; corner cupboards sometimes had arch tops and shell-carved vaulted interiors. Imported English and Dutch decorative tiles began to cover the brick facings of fireplaces. The whole tradition was of course English, but a distinctive American style was being developed by creative American builders and cabinet makers. Color was in the deep tones of rust red, blues, greens and ochres already described as having been used in the earlier period, and these set off the wood trim handsomely against oyster-white plastered walls. Many of these rooms might be described as Georgian, which indeed they were in feeling,

* Bolection—A type of heavy molding framing a fireplace.

5

particularly the later ones of this period which formed a transition into the following style.

GEORGIAN-COLONIAL

The middle, the third quarter, and part of the last quarter of the 18th century constituted the era of the Georgian style in this country. This became a highly developed period in decoration marked by more elaborate classic features such as fluted pilasters with Corinthian capitols, higher ceilings, elaborate cornices, pediments, arches, panels with broken corners, high relief carving inspired by the English wood carver Grinling Gibbons, and more decoration in general. The scenic wallpapers which appeared in the more handsome and formal rooms, were usually imported from France or China, though stenciling was used in their place for borders or overall decoration in simple houses. Also, there are examples of landscape wall decorations done in rather primitive style by native artists. Paint colors in this period became far less somber and dark, and trim was often painted a light clear tone of blue, green, or gold. Chippendale was the dominating influence in furniture design during this period, though Queen Anne motifs persisted throughout the 18th century in many localities. Distinctive American Chippendale furniture was developed which differed from English pieces and in many cases outstripped them in beauty.

FEDERAL

The Federal Period includes the last two decades of the 18th century and a generous decade of the 19th. The heavier Georgian gave way to more delicate lines and detail, fine fluting * and reeding in pilasters and cornices, lighter, smaller moldings, fan-shaped lights, slender window muntins, and putty mold decoration in place of heavy carving in garland, figure and floral designs. Much of the work of this period was inspired by the Adam brothers, but a truly individual American style emerged when we became an independent nation of Federated States. Furniture in the style of Adam,

* Fluting—Consists of narrow, concave grooves. Reeding is the opposite, or convex ridges.

6

Hepplewhite, Sheraton, and Duncan Phyfe was used against this background. Paint on trim became light and pale, often in two tones. White and soft pastel shades were used at this time, as well as pearl grey, putty color, and grey containing a hint of green, mauve or tan.

Some examples in the later Federal style might be called early Empire, though classical motifs born of Greece and Rome, by way of the Renaissance, began to be evident well before 1800. As the Federal style continued to develop we find classic free-standing columns, and details such as the acanthus leaf, the honeysuckle, and lyre motifs. Curved lines in furniture were inspired by the French Directoire. This was delicate and graceful at first, and the best pieces by Duncan Phyfe and other cabinet makers of his school belong to this group. From our own new life as an independent nation, influenced principally by Adam and the French, we created this, our most individual contribution to design, the style known as Federal.

POST-FEDERAL

The fifth and last grouping (after 1815–1820) shows the unfortunate but natural decline of taste following the peak of an artistic development. The Empire period began to replace the finer Federal about 1820 and, together with the Greek revival influence, caused a gradual deterioration of design in this country. Later Empire soon developed heavy moldings, overloaded curves, and a generally coarser appearance, as the delicacy of preceding periods disappeared. The Victorian interiors which followed were ornate, and though overburdened with plush, fringes, and questionable statuary, had a certain elegance and beauty.

From this time taste degenerated in New England into later and nameless periods sometimes associated with General Ulysses S. Grant, who could not in any way have been held responsible, poor man, as he was completely occupied with military affairs at the time and not with the design of fringed plush portières. Eventually things degenerated to a point of meaningless ornament and knick-knackery about which the less said the better.

7

FURNITURE

The answer to the question of what furniture to use in period interiors such as those described above, might seem obvious—one should use pieces in the styles of corresponding date. This is not as simple as it sounds, because the changes in furniture design did not parallel literally and exactly in time the architectural changes. Thus we see Queen Anne furniture made and used throughout most of the 18th century, and simple ladder-back chairs, which were made shortly after 1700, continued to appear just as long. Surely home owners, such as you and I, did not discard all of their old furniture when new styles came in, and, no doubt, they also used pieces in the new style even in interiors of earlier date. Transition pieces are perfectly at home in interiors of the foregoing or following period. Well designed antiques can also be used against a background of purely modern architecture. Rooms of extraordinary charm have been created in this way.

Of equal importance is the matter of harmonizing the *character* of background and furniture. Thus a formal and elaborate Chippendale piece is set off to greater advantage against a Georgian or Federal background, and a primitive interior seems to demand simple pieces whether of early or late make. For instance, a later simple ladder-back chair, a Windsor, which was a type made from about 1725 on, or even a Hitchcock of 19th-century make, is quite appropriate with exposed beams and simple pine sheathing, whose charm would be hidden by, for example, carved mahogany and silk brocatelle hangings.

Therefore, it is quite apparent that the decorating problem resolves itself approximately into the two subjects: period, in which we may take wide latitude, and suitability of character.

When it comes to matters of taste no book of this sort can hope to do more than make a few suggestions, many in negative form. For instance: no piece of furniture belongs in a corner except a corner-shaped piece. This includes corner cupboards, roundabout or corner chairs, and occasionally a small table of rounded shape. In fact, avoid putting pieces

8

across corners unless they fit. A right angle is a sound thing and not to be treated with disrespect.

In treating old pine sheathing or floors, or in imitating them, avoid a strong yellow or "pumpkin" tone. As it ages pine takes on a soft grey-tan shade of far greater beauty. Do not indulge in the fad for "knotty" pine which has a purely commercial origin. The best wood always has been, and continues to be, that containing the fewest knots.

Give serious consideration to the fact that a kitchen in which much time is spent need not have the cold appearance of a laboratory. Old wood, color, and decoration are not incompatible with an electric dish washer.

For first-hand knowledge of color, style, and materials many of our museums and well restored houses which can be visited, offer great funds of information. Excellent reproductions of furniture, textiles, wallpapers, and period colors in paint are manufactured today and will go far toward helping one recreate a period room. There is a revival of interest in the crafts, and instruction may easily be obtained from books on all subjects from the stenciling of walls to painted tinware or braided and hooked rugs. Photo murals can be an excellent and very personal substitute for scenic wallpapers. Doing things oneself is not only economical but gives an added personal value to one's surroundings.

The following résumé of period furniture in New England is brief in the extreme, and in no way pretends to complete coverage of a large and interesting subject. Further study will lead to infinite and fascinating ramifications. But our hope is to give simple guidance to those who aim to preserve the best of our past, and integrate its feeling and atmosphere into their homes today.

EARLY AMERICAN

The 17th-century pieces of furniture brought to this country were largely Elizabethan (or Tudor) and Jacobean in style. These were copied or adapted by American craftsmen in the woods at hand, which included oak, pine, ash and maple. The Elizabethan was very heavy and ponderous. Refectory tables had great bulb or "melon"-turned legs, and benches and

9

chests were weighty. The Jacobean which followed was somewhat lighter and more adaptable to present-day living. Rooms in the earliest houses were small, and furniture sparse and often designed to save space. Thus developed folding press beds (so-called because they fitted into a press or cupboard), demountable trestle tables, as well as drop-leaf, gate-leg, and butterfly tables. The latter took their name from the shape of the supports which held up the drop leaves. The long trestle table was put up at meal times with perhaps a wainscot or Brewster chair at the head for the master of the household, while the rest of the family sat upon joined stools and benches. When the meal was over the table was demounted or folded to one side, and the family living continued about the fire in this main room or "hall," in which was done the cooking, dining, work of the household, and where some members of the family probably slept. Chests were essential pieces of furniture, as linen, clothing and other possessions were kept in them. They may have been plain or paneled, scratch-carved, painted, or carved in low relief. Some were developed with one drawer, or even two, below the top section. There were also chests of the Hadley, Connecticut, type with split spindle decoration and applied moldings. Some prosperous families may have owned court or press cupboards, decorated in Tudor style with bulbous turned posts, intricate panels, and applied turned pieces and carving. Sometimes there were also touches of paint. The press cupboard was entirely, or almost entirely enclosed. The court cupboard was usually open above and below to display ornaments and plate. Looking glasses were small, simple, and very rare. Lighting was obtained from hanging iron "Betty" lamps, or candles in wooden or iron floor stands, or in pewter candlesticks.

The family may have owned a "Bible box," or small slope-front writing box, or a desk-on-frame, as well as a simple corner cupboard, sometimes scroll-trimmed, to hold treasured household pewter utensils. Beds were simple frames with laced ropes to hold the bedding and often of the folding type already mentioned. Other pieces known here in the years before and shortly after 1700 included Cromwellian chairs with turned posts, upholstered seats and low rectangular upholstered backs, Brewster and Carver chairs with heavy turned posts and spindles in back and arms (named respectively for two of the Pilgrim fathers, William Brewster and John Carver, who presumably used this type), early ladder-backs, Carolean chairs with Flemish scroll-carved backs and turned legs. Some of these were "bannister" backs—chairs with upright slats resembling bannisters, usually painted black and with rush seats. Others had caned seats and backs. There were also some day-beds in the Carolean style. The simpler pieces of local make included pine settles, hutch tables and chair tables, tavern tables with stretchers and extended tops, candle stands, open and closed shelf cupboards, pine slant-top desks, as well as a variety of lighting, cooking, and fireside implements. Skins of animals were used on furniture and perhaps floors, and materials were homespun and home-dyed.

The Windsor chair, a comfortable and charming style, with shaped wooden saddle seat and slender spindles in back and arms, first appeared in Philadelphia about 1725. It was such a popular style that it was made until the last quarter of the 19th century.

The William and Mary style first appeared in this country about 1680 adding a Dutch influence to furniture design. Some of its characteristics are the double hood, or double arch that capped cabinets, crossed stretchers bracing chair and table legs, flat stretchers in curving shapes, trumpet turned and inverted cap legs, flattened ball feet, and the use of burl woods on the face of finer pieces. Chairs had high, sometimes carved crested backs, Flemish scroll legs, turned legs and caned or rush seats. Flat topped highboys with trumpet turned legs appeared, as well as lowboys or dressing tables. These had brass single drop pulls of pear shape or "tear drop" design. There were simple carved or painted looking glasses, desks with ball or turnip feet, and possibly in prosperous homes tall clocks of inlaid walnut, as well as cabinets with double hood tops. The comfortable upholstered wing chair appeared, and materials such as damasks, velvets and embroideries in rich primary colors. The more elaborate of these furnishings would be out of place in a truly primitive early interior and are more suitable, of course, against the later background of boxed-in beams and paneled fireplace ends.

11

MID-COLONIAL

In our Mid-Colonial Period, beginning with the second quarter of the 18th century, the Queen Anne style had already appeared in this country. Its chief characteristic, the Cabriole leg, which has a sort of gracefully bow-legged line, dates from about 1730, though the transition between furniture styles began earlier. Life became somewhat easier and the comfort of up-holstered pieces included wing chairs, sofas, and stools. Arm chairs and side chairs had vase or fiddle-shape splats set in tall backs curved for comfort. Feet were of the types known as pad, scroll, club, and duck, with ball-and-claw feet appearing at the end of the period. Chests and desks sometimes had bracket feet; there were lowboys and highboys closely resembling those made in the William and Mary period except for the curved legs. High secretaries and chests of drawers appeared, tea tables, small stands, fancy looking glasses, slant-top desks and tester beds. There was veneering, inlay, lacquering and japanning on more elaborate pieces. Materials such as linens and chintzes were used, as well as needle-point and embroideries in bright rich colors. Toward the end of the period pieces became fretted and carved, gilded or painted, and claw-and-ball feet and scallop shell ornament showed a clear trend toward the Georgian. But the simple native American Queen Anne type of furniture persisted until well toward the end of the 18th century.

GEORGIAN-COLONIAL

Toward the middle of the 18th century Queen Anne furniture began to take on the Georgian influence, and from this time to about 1780—the period we are calling Georgian-Colonial—there developed in this country a style of furniture usually called Chippendale, after the greatest of the Georgian designers. Much of it was only inspired by his ideas, and actually developed by imaginative American craftsmen with individuality of their own. Mahogany was the favorite wood, though walnut, curly maple, pop-lar and pine were used, particularly by country craftsmen. Straight lines were much in evidence, and instead of rounded backs, the chairs had straighter tops rising to a pair of ear-like shapes at each corner. The splats

12

were pierced in fanciful designs; there were ribband backs, imitating elaborately coiled and woven ribbons (or ribbands) as well as carved ladderbacks; legs were straight or cabriole with claw-and-ball, lion's paw or French feet. Settees and sofas followed the same designs, or were fully upholstered with high arms rolling back to each side. There were fine wing chairs, card tables, tilt-top tables with pie-crust or scalloped edges, great bonnet-top secretaries, highboys, lowboys, cabinets, knee-hole and slope-front desks, chests of drawers, mirrors, and ornaments of many kinds. Hardware was of pierced brass, often Chinese in feeling. Large and beautifully carved pieces of mahogany made a handsome showing in the high-ceilinged architectural interiors, with gleaming brass and crystal, and perhaps rich hangings of gold or crimson damask. Other materials used were East India prints, toiles-de-Jouy (a printed linen made in France), brocatelles, chintzes, and hand-blocked or printed linens. Furniture known as "blockfront," because the frontal pieces were fashioned in different planes carefully carved from a single piece of wood, existed in the form of desks, chests of drawers, and exceptionally handsome secretaries and cabinets. This unique style was purely an American development, and represents possibly our finest contribution to the art of the cabinetmaker.

FEDERAL

Little or no furniture was made in this country from the designs of the Adam brothers. Yet the name Adam remains one of the greatest influences of our Federal period because it inspired most of the best work of the English cabinet makers Hepplewhite and Sheraton. And they, together with the American Duncan Phyfe, were definitely the designers whose work and style were most prevalent at this time. The other influence which had much to do with forming this charming, useable and truly American style of furniture was the French Directoire, which added curved lines of delicate grace. Duncan Phyfe and other craftsmen were inspired by these French models.

Taste in furniture turned from the ornate Georgian, and from its Chinese forms, toward delicacy and classic detail. Hepplewhite used clean-cut

13

lines, simple forms and straight tapering legs. He used mahogany and satin-wood, various inlays and painted panels. Most of his chairs had shield-shaped, oval or hoop backs, with splats in designs of the Prince of Wales feathers, vases, lyres, and other patterns. Among the decorative details are found floral swags, pendant husks, and clusters of wheat. The front legs were straight and tapering, fluted, or reeded, with spade feet. The back legs had a rear-sweeping curve. Hepplewhite chests of drawers had curved bracket feet, and straight or bowed fronts. Sideboards with serpentine fronts, with cupboards and drawers, sofas with numerous slender legs and no stretchers, various tables including card tables and the Pembroke drop-leaf type, four-post bed, desks and secretaries, tall clocks, in fact almost every article of household furniture was made in the Hepplewhite style.

Sheraton, also inspired by Adam as well as by Louis XVI styles, and Hepplewhite himself, combined certain features of each into a very useable, informal style. Many Hepplewhite and Sheraton pieces resemble each other so closely as to be indistinguishable. It is said that a Sheraton sideboard often had inward curving ends, whereas a Hepplewhite would be convex. Sheraton chairs are easy to distinguish for their square backs with straight lines, filled with somewhat geometric shapes, diamonds, straight spindles, urn or lyre splats, or the so-called "cathedral" back. Sometimes vase shapes appeared in legs and posts, though they were usually straight and tapered, square or round, reeded or fluted, with a spade foot. In the Sheraton style we find approximately the same articles of household furniture as in the Hepplewhite style.

Federal furniture with French Directoire influence is commonly re-ferred to as the Duncan Phyfe style, though there were many cabinetmakers who made this type, distinguished by the curved line. These are character-istics of this Phyfe-Federal style: chairs having inward curving legs; grace-fully curved benches with swan's-neck arms; sofas showing these same curves and carved frames; dainty sewing tables; four-foot pedestal tables; the lyre motif in chair backs and sofa ends; beds with twisted carved posts, carved eagles and shields as well as reeding and fluting for decoration. Painted "fancy" chairs and benches with rush seats appeared at this time.

14

The Hitchcock chair, painted and decorated with stencils, was not made until 1820 but had a long life and is still a most useful and suitable piece of furniture in an interior of Federal or later style.

Materials used in Federal interiors ranged from dressy taffetas, satins and moirés, Chinese silks and embroidered mulls, to simpler printed cottons.

POST-FEDERAL

Because the Federal period was one of fine and good taste, our best and our very own, it is rather saddening to relate the downfall of general design which followed. The French Empire style began to be popular in this country about 1820. Together with the Greek Revival it dominated design for awhile, and though some pieces are very good, the use of machinery after 1825 caused the finer craftsmanship to disappear. A general coarsening set in, and while there is much to be said about the furniture of this time, and all that followed during the Victorian era, this book is not designed to cover it, nor, I am afraid, is the inclination of the author.

INDEX

Figures in heavy type indicate the number of the illustration. Lightface figures indicate page number of text.

17

20

INDEX

22

*Halls
and
Stairways*

1

1. One entered the earliest homes on these shores through heavy doors, solidly built, and bolted against the elements or even more threatening marauders. These may have been constructed of two layers of heavy planks, laid against each other horizontally on the interior, and vertically on the outside, which is nail studded, as in the Bubier Mansion, Marblehead, Mass. (circa 1695). This door, a restoration from the late 17th century, has arch top, great original hinges which pivot in their own handwrought sockets, a huge lock applied to the surface, and no decoration beyond a simple beading where door and wall are joined in one flat surface. The steep narrow stairway on the right is boxed in behind simple vertical pine sheathing, joined with feathered edges. The chairs are a pair of French ones from Lorraine, suitable in style and period. Horizontal sheathing on the left shows it to have been an outside wall. To the left is a most practical powder-room, tactfully indicated by an old powder horn hanging above the door.

2

3

2. Here the beams have been boxed in and the stairway constructed with charming simple post and rail and turned balusters. The heavy paneled door is a double one, opening in the center. The slat-back high chair may have been used at a desk. (Mission House, Stockbridge, Mass., 1739)

3. A steep old stairway turns within its restricted space. The old chair and table of early period are suitable furnishings. Pieces of pewter and an arrangement of driftwood and dried berries are perfect decoration against the old pine sheathing. The oldest part of this house in Salem, Mass., dates from 1651.

4   5

4. The entrance door of the Frary House, Deerfield, Massachusetts, is bolted top and bottom, and further strengthened by a wooden bar. Here the stairway makes two turns with landings, though remaining steep and narrow. The niche under the stairs might hold a conveniently lit mirror and table, while the bench which fills the rest of the space would be convenient for storage under the lid. (Frary House, Deerfield, Mass., early 1680's)

5. Beveled rectangular panels and turned post and balusters embellish this handsome stair hall. A pair of early Queen Anne Spanish-foot chairs flank an unusual gate-leg table against the wall. Oriental rugs, candle sconces, and an early engraving further mark this interior as one of taste and comfort. Spacious though spacesaving, it is a perfect model of this mid-Colonial type of hall. (Parson Ashley House, Deerfield, Mass., Circa 1730)

6

7

8   9

6. A sunlit upper stair hall in an Essex, Mass., house contains a desk-on-frame, and an early grandfather's clock. The stair rail and balusters, and simple door frames are typical of the period following the first primitive type of construction. Such an upper landing makes a cheerful study or work-room.

7. More spacious proportions with a wider, though still simple stairway are shown in this hallway. The wood floor is interestingly painted in squares to imitate black and white marble. (Tobias Lear House, Portsmouth, N. H., circa 1740)

8. Elaborately turned balusters, arched and Palladian windows, higher ceilings and more elaborate moldings came to the American house with the Georgian influence. The high recessed window supplies seating space, as well as fine lighting, and the walls are covered with a paper of old design. (Salem, Mass., 1748)

9. An example of how an upper stair hall can add practically another room to the house. The desk, window-seat and conveniently built-in bookcases are all ideas for putting a small space to pleasant use. (Salem, Mass., 1760)

27

10.

10. A recessed window supplies fine lighting from the side. The scenic paper is magnificent, and sufficient decoration. (Moffatt-Ladd House, Portsmouth, N. H., 1763)

11. Fine mahogany balusters are silhouetted against this handsomely architectural stair hall. The tall window gives the fine lighting so needed in a stairway. (Wentworth-Gardner House, Portsmouth, N. H., 1760)

12. Elaborate cornice with dentil molding, handsomely paneled wainscot and doors, frame a scenic wall paper. This stunning decorative style of the third quarter of the 18th century is easily adapted by using photo murals of your own choosing, or panels of decorative scenic paper obtainable today. (Moffatt-Ladd House, Portsmouth, N. H., 1763)

13

14

15

16

17

18

13. In the late 18th century and Federal period grace and delicacy of detail reflect the influence of the Adam brothers and other designers of this school. In a fine old mansion in Portsmouth, N. H., (1799), we see a scroll decoration on each stair end. This is a development of the same motif that appeared in heavier form in preceding years. But the delicately curving stairway whose slender rail soars aloft in one fine sweep, is distinctly a development of this period.

14. The arched doorways in the same house are simple but elegant, with incised carvings of rosettes and flutings for decoration, rather than the heavy embossed ornament of the Georgian period. The fanlight was a natural solution for filling the archway of these door frames. A pair of Queen Anne chairs flanks the front door whose arch is tied by a keystone to the cornice above.

15. Still very architectural in style, a rectangular door frames another view of the stairs. Here again is visible a variety of delicate ornamentation in the woodwork. The curved shield-back settee was designed for the space it so perfectly fills.

16. A bird's-eye view of the snail-like curves shows the full beauty of this same staircase, terminating in the accented period of the newel post below.

17. Governor Gore paved the hallway of his spacious mansion with squares of marble. Ample lights surround the door, and the furnishings of the period include Chinese porcelains. (Gore Place, Waltham, Mass., 1802)

18. Light and graceful decoration, typical of Samuel McIntire, Salem's famous architect and wood carver, ornaments this Federal hallway. The grandfather's clock stands with dignity against a paper of contemporary design. (Salem, Circa 1805)

19

19. A lower ceiled hall at Gore Place is paved with black and white marble which may be imitated with inlaid linoleum in a more simple house. The shallow arch in the wall containing a "grandmother's" clock is a happy note. The furniture of the period is delicate in design, in keeping with the architecture.

20. This stair hall in Salem, Mass., shows the transition to the Empire period in its rather heavy, bracketed arch, though the Federal style persists in the details. Homelike and spacious, all too few builders would give it "house room" today. (1815)

21

Living Rooms

and Libraries

21. In the Early American house some of the pine sheathing was joined at the seams by a "shadow" molding. Latches were of wood, and in such primitive interiors the beams and great fireplace lintels were exposed. Here a table-chair at the left and settle at the right of the chimney carry skins, such as were used for coverings in the early days. Bunches of herbs hang to dry near the fire, and though simple and stark, the atmosphere of this room is homelike and warm. (Harlow House, Plymouth, Mass., 1677)

24

22. An open door in the pine sheathing over a fireplace in the Major John Bradford House, Kingston, Mass., (1674), shows space against the brick chimney convenient for storage or for hiding valuables. Jacobean furniture is exemplified in the tables with turned legs and stretchers, and the primitive four-legged stools.

23. The library of this old house in Marblehead, Mass. (1695), was originally the kitchen. The best pine sheathing of this kind was always clear of knots, so it is wise to avoid the so-called "knotty-pine" boards, a fashion of purely commercial basis. The natural tone of the wood in this room is deep grey-tan due to its age, and far lovelier than the yellow, or "pumpkin" pine stain so often used in imitations. A touch of brightest vermilion is used in the indentations of the dentil trim joining sheathing and fireplace lintel. This is echoed in the lining and shelves of the bookcases. An old lantern wired for electricity hangs from the beam at the left.

24. In the same room recessed book shelves are separated by a simple batten door with old "H" hinges which leads to an insulated wine closet containing a small sink for bar use. The space above the door is utilized as a shelf for small leather bindings. The old provincial French cabinet hides radio and record-player, while the French *panetière* (a bread or food safe) on it contains the loudspeaker. Curtains are of coarsely woven natural linen thread, trimmed only with a line of vermilion gimp. Ceiling boards and beams are waxed but not shiny. A milk bench makes a convenient coffee table.

25

26

27

25. Boards which formed a low wainscot were used to face the book shelves in this same room. The door at the left is almost invisible, cut in one with the pine sheathing. The mixture of Early American with French Provincial furniture whose woods are the same tone, combined with a modern sofa of harmonious lines, shows clearly the possibility of mingling periods old and new with comfort and charm.

26. A beautifully restored early house in Old Deerfield, Mass. (circa 1710), contains rare old boards in the sheathing remarkable for their width. The fireplace lintel is exposed as are the beams and ceiling, and though this is an early type of interior it is handsome enough to house furniture of more elegant standards, such as the gold brocaded Queen Anne settees by the fireplace. A rarely fine needlepoint pole screen stands near the chimney.

27. Small tables and candle stands hold many brass candlesticks actually used for illumination in the same room (it has no electricity). The mellow glow of candlelight alone must be lived with to be appreciated. Curtains are of old Crewel-work in warm rich colors. The early ladder-back chair with mushroom knobs is probably a century the senior in age of the painted Windsor rocker. The early spinet at the right bears some beautiful examples of old American silver. Above it hangs one fine Chippendale mirror. Another is above a William and Mary lowboy. Hooked rugs, though later in period are perfectly harmonious in such a room.

28

29

30

28. The Derby House in Salem, Mass., (1761) is an example of a much earlier style. Obviously merchant Richard Derby had his house copied from drawings of an earlier period. This parlor shows fine examples of raised panels and bolection moldings of the Mid-Colonial style. The walls are painted in rich colors, and have a deep red molding around the fireplace openings throughout the house, perhaps in imitation of their dark marble originals in England. The recessed windows have paneled fold-back shutters to be closed at night, and a shallow window seat. Here a desk-on-frame stands at the right. The chairs are of the type known as bannister-backs. The cupboard, left of the fireplace, could house radio or television, books or china.

29. Simple classic architectural features which appeared after 1725 are expressed in this Essex, Mass., arched corner cupboard with fluted pilasters. Off-white rough plaster walls (sometimes the result of mixing sand with the plaster) contrast with wood trim usually painted in deep rich colors—India red, deep blue, green or earth colors. An early butter-fly table, bannister-back armchair, and a winged rocker form part of the furnishings.

30. A fine example of how a paneled fireplace end can "make" a room is shown in the Mid-Colonial Mission House (1739) in Stockbridge, Mass. The Queen Anne wing chair is covered suitably in beautiful crewel-work. On the stone hearth stands a ratchet candle stand, a foot warmer and kettle.

31

32

31. Vertical panels rather than horizontal have been used over the fireplace, showing the effort made for variety in this house. The oak chest is of the Hadley type with split turned pieces for decoration.

32. A paneled dado and recessed window seats, together with a simple cornice molding, frame the papered walls of this room. The paper is an interesting design, taken from the covering of an old bandbox. It is one of a series of authentic designs sold under the name of "Heritage Papers." Before the 18th-century desk stands a "roundabout" or corner chair. The side chairs are simple American Chippendale. (Frary House, Deerfield, Mass., circa 1688)

40

33

33. The exact period of this room is far from defined, but it is clear it has been put together by the hand of a master. The simple beveled panels are painted an ochre brown, and the curtains are turkey red. An octagonal drop-leaf table stands in the center. At the side is a fine small pedestal table and a drop-leaf Pembroke table, both in curly maple. The so-called Martha Washington armchair is placed near an early Franklin wood-burning stove built into the fireplace. All ornaments are original pieces. (The Franklin Room in Beauport, East Gloucester, Mass.)

34. A beautiful block-front Chippendale secretary, made about 1775, and at one time owned by the poet Longfellow, a Chippendale armchair, and a shelf clock (on the right) form part of the handsome furnishings of this room. Every candlestick and ornament is authentic. (Parson Ashley House, Deerfield, Mass.)

41

35

36

35. An elaborately handsome mansion of the third quarter of the 18th century contains Georgian rooms on the grand scale. Here we see a marble-faced paneled and carved fireplace, deep paneled dados and intricate cornice detail. Scenic papers for large rooms of this type are obtainable today, but photomurals made from your favorite pictures would be a constant pleasure. (Lee Mansion, Marblehead, Mass., 1768)

36. Each wall space carries a different decorative landscape paper of classic feeling, resembling the style of Piranesi's famous engravings of Rome. Their tones are warm greys and the woodwork is painted a cream-grey. Rich green damask curtains hang at the tall windows. Here we see a Queen Anne wing chair near the fireplace, upholstered in the same material as the hangings. Beside it is placed a candle stand and in the background a Queen Anne lowboy stands between two Chippendale ladder-back chairs. (Lee Mansion, Marblehead, Mass., 1768)

37

37. The Octagon Room in Beauport is startling, original, and beautiful, with walls painted eggplant-black picked out with fine lines of vermilion. Against this, lightest golden maple furniture, a quantity of lacquer red tole ware, and floral curtains are more than effective. Pedimented doors carrying red tole urns, the center octagonal table, Chippendable and Federal chairs, a red screen, silhouettes in old frames, hooked rugs—it sounds like a mixed salad indeed, but in reality has been masterfully organized into a room of great beauty. (Beauport, East Gloucester, Mass.)

38. At Beauport also is this library in a tower. A gallery above, cleverly curved book shelves, the windows a fantasy of three pointed arches curtained in carved wood from an old hearse (yes!) show again the originality of the master-decorator and collector responsible for this house.

39. Fine gilt cornices surmount the windows in this Salem, Mass., house, built in 1816. A handsome gilt 18th-century mirror hung between them further enriches the decorative scheme. The paper and woodwork are a soft green, the hangings, apricot. The window seats are small separate benches in each recess. The glass shaded lamp with glinting prisms is placed in the exact center of the table. Symmetry and balance in the basic features of a scheme of decoration assure a sound and harmonious background, no matter how irrelevantly you may choose to place surface features and small ornaments.

40. The oval drawing room of Governor Gore's great Federal mansion (1802-1804) in Waltham, Mass., has a paneled dado and tall recessed windows within which the sectional blinds fold away. The beauty of the high curving walls is unmarred, as the paper is of the simplest possible design and the window curtains hang in straight undraped folds. A beautiful crystal candelabra is the only ornament on the Chippendale table before the window.

41. This house in Salem, Mass., was designed by Samuel McIntire in 1804. Somewhat later is the style of the immensely tall pier glass whose crested top echoes the glint of gilded cornices from which fall heavy straight curtains at the high windows. The low French console with marble top is the correct base for such a glass, and its French feeling is echoed in the curving lines of the table within the window. In the mirror is reflected McIntire's fireplace.

39

40

41

42   **43**

42. The friendly grouping of Chippendale table and chairs before the sofa in this early 19th-century Federal parlor is charming and worth noting; at least as comfortable as the usual modern low coffee table in such a spot and possibly more so. Here old crystal wine carafes and glasses, and chair seats of early embroidery, complete the authenticity of the picture. The rich crimson hangings are interestingly made, to be released by a cord and dropped straight over the windows at night. The symmetry of a single curtain on each side, with dropping tassel, framing the center group of card table and a banjo clock, shows again the importance of balance and symmetrical design in an interior. The central brass chandelier is earlier in period, and cleverly electrified with very tiny bulbs which give a light resembling candle flame. (Stebbins House, Deerfield, Mass., 1799-1815)

43. The Stebbins House also shows a small, pale but sophisticated interior with Aubusson carpet, crystal chandelier, plaster-decorated ceiling in the Adam tradition, and late 18th- and early 19th-century furniture. The walls are palest pink, the thin white India mull window curtains are surmounted by brocade swags in 19th-century style, and a fine old pink luster tea set rests on the center table. Tones in the brocade swags and the rug are predominantly *bois de rose*, blue and gold.

44

Dining Rooms
and Kitchens

44. This charming old hearth is replete with ideas for your own informal cellar game room or cottage kitchen. A great wood lintel rests in the massive stone construction of the chimney in this old cellar kitchen. The floor is also paved with stones, and the thick stone foundation wall of the house is visible on the right. Crude benches of split logs and primitive boards are grouped around the primitive table upon which stands an immense old burl bowl. Left of the fire hangs a wooden bread shovel for removing loaves from the oven which opens beside it, its wooden removable door resting on the floor below. Ladles, forks, pots, skewers, a roaster and turning spit are close at hand. The long wooden bar above may be swung out and a curtain hung upon it to keep out draughts from the entry door.

45

46

47

45. Vertical sheathing, exposed construction and small lead-paned windows (restored) mark this Marlboro, Mass., home as a very early one. We find a four-post bed in the room used for dining and living purposes. This was customary at the time and provided warm sleeping quarters for a guest or members of the family. This one is dressed in a colorful old material forming curtains which could be closed at night. The center table is an early drop-leaf duckfoot type. Bread, cheese and wine are invitingly at hand for a snack.

46. A great room, or living "hall" in the same house offers ideas for a combination living and dining room of today. The great stone chimney with furniture invitingly grouped about it, is partially separated from the dining end by a jog in the wall. Here the long table may be used for working or reading by day, for dining at night.

47. In this day of simple living, when many of us choose to cook and dine within the same four walls, efficient working space is in no way incompatible with beauty. In this kitchen-dining room, cupboard doors near the fireplace conceal a multitude of practical articles. An old drop-leaf table at the left would be perfect for preparation of food, while on the shelves above it stands an array of pewter mugs and dishes, to be replaced by your own favorite pots and pans. The round dining table stands in the foreground surrounded by slat-back chairs. Picture in your imagination a modern stove and sink hidden behind the settle at your right and you have a perfect set-up for modern living with old world charm. The open hearth is an indispensable feature for cheer, and charcoal broiling. (Hathaway House, Salem, Mass., 1682)

48

49

50

48. Primitive stools and a hutch table may not offer the utmost in luxury, but are worth considering for practical small family use in a restricted space. The simplicity of the space-saving dresser, here lined with old pewter, is perfectly adaptable to modern needs, as are the table and chest along the wall, and the implements hung on old nails along the horizontal wall sheathing. The large shelf suspended from the beams is another idea for saving space. (John Ward House, Salem, Mass., 1684)

49. Windsor chairs, stools and benches all may be used for sitting at this old tavern table lighted from above by a pierced iron lantern of early date. The simple corner cupboard at the left, small wall cupboard and small cabinet at the end of the table, are convenient and at hand, as suitable and useful today as in the past, as are the printed calico curtains at the small-paned windows, and hooked rugs on the floor. (Beauport, East Gloucester, Mass.)

50. A great settle stands beside the hearth in this early kitchen-living room of the same house, almost partitioning off the section where stands the dining table, lighted by an old candle stand, surrounded by Windsor chairs and benches. A large old dresser, whose drawers, cupboard, and shelves hold about everything necessary for use nearby, stands at the right. At the end are two cupboards between which opens the half-door of a small bar, lighted by a window opposite. Across this flat-topped door may be passed food and drink, an excellent idea to adapt for the modern house in these times of informal entertaining.

51

51

51. This old brick chimney is completely exposed, showing unusual arched brick construction above the lintel which supports the hearth in the second floor. The bare construction and rough plaster walls are relieved by a strip of old needlepoint hanging between batten door and window. An old tin chandelier hangs above the gate-leg table, which is covered with a red and white woven cloth, much later in period but entirely suitable in this room. (Stephen Daniel House, Salem, Mass., 1667-1756)

52. This handsome formal dining room (circa 1710), in a Deerfield, Mass., house, contrasts with the more primitive farm kitchens and "halls" illustrated before. Beautiful Queen Anne chairs, their seats covered with fine old embroidered material, surround an early gate-leg table. The feathered sheathing is simple and early, and the brass chandelier is typical of the early 18th century. The fireplace has an oven built in at the right, useful for storing wood. Above is an ingenious use of space between panels and sloping chimney for a small closed cupboard and open shelves to hold decorative and useful articles.

53. This old kitchen with horizontal sheathing, inside wooden shutters and exposed beams might well be used as a model for a contemporary kitchen-dining room. On the hearth stands a roaster while the mechanism of an old spit-jack is seen above. The early cupboard against the wall, old hutch table and early chairs are at home in the surroundings. Small-paned windows are in correct scale. (Parson Ashley House, Deerfield, Mass., circa 1730)

54   **55**

54. After the first period of exposed construction, simple beveled paneling was introduced, as in this dado, and beams were boxed in. In this Mid-Colonial house an old dresser, with cupboard door made of one rectangular panel, holds pewter, wooden and earthware objects. The chairs are an American transition type with Spanish feet and Chippendale backs. Simple checkered curtains hang at the small-paned windows. A perfect dining-room for the small house today. (Mission House, Stockbridge, Mass., 1739)

55. Windsor chairs and pewter plates invite dining beside a cheery fire. The table is also a work table with drawers and space for bowls or other implements. (Lee Mansion, Marblehead, Mass., 1768)

56. For a large party, an unusual arrangement of sectional tables placed in horseshoe shape enables guests to enjoy the fire without being uncomfortably close to it. Service is easy from the inside of the curve. Light is from a series of old candlesticks only. (Hartwell Farm, Lincoln, Mass., 1636-1639)

57. This low ceilinged old house of about 1700, in Marblehead, has simple paneling and boxed beams added a few decades later. From the center beam hangs a detachable small brass chandelier of the early 18th century. The early French oak table, in style resembling the Jacobean, carries a spoon rack and a three-piece Britanniaware tea set of the 19th century. The mirror is American Chippendale. Small-paned heavy-muntined windows give authentic character, and the transparent curtains of linen gauze, outlined in simple dark blue braid, are hung on wooden rods by cloth loops, according to the custom of the period. The large braided rug of blue, brown, dull red and beige harmonizes with the "India" red stain of the woodwork. The plastered walls are a happy off-white, obtained by using sand in the plaster. The old wide pine floor boards are a ripe brown.

56

57

58

59

58. Beauty and utility can and should be combined in a room where the modern-day housewife spends much of her time. The waxed cupboard doors in this Marblehead kitchen are made of old pine sheathing with iron "H" hinges and latches. Counters are of hard birch at the level of the stove. Old copper saucepans, earthenware vessels, and a bright vermilion painted spice box for bread, are not only in constant use but form a fine color scheme against natural wood and green walls. Three rounded shelves to hold spices fill the angle between cupboard and wall.

59. The side casements of this window in the same kitchen allow ventilation while matching the heavy muntined panes throughout the house. The lamp is made of an old rum jug, and the early French table and chairs offer inviting possibilities for a kitchen meal when the dining room is not in use. Walls are sage green, wood unpainted but darkened with age, and the rubber tile floor dull brick red.

60

60. Toward the middle of the 18th century Georgian styles appeared. In the dining room of an old house in Salem, (1748), is a fireplace with pilasters and broken rectangular panel. The fine pedestal table and Hepplewhite chairs are appropriate though of later period. The crested pier glass between the windows adds a golden glint with the rich brocade curtains. Mahogany, brass and glass, oriental rugs and silver are all in keeping with the developing luxury of higher ceiled rooms and more sophisticated living.

61

62

61. This Bilbao mirror, veneered with sheets of marble and gilt-trimmed, is of a type imported from Spain in the 18th century. It hangs above a Queen Anne lowboy between two tall recessed windows whose damask curtains hang in straight folds from beneath scalloped valances. A knife box, glass decanters, goblets, and a flip glass stand upon the lowboy. The curtains in this Georgian dining-room are a beautiful true red against woodwork painted a strong, light, almost turquoise blue. (Lee Mansion, Marblehead, Mass., 1768)

62. An arched niche seems made for the Hepplewhite sideboard, while Chippendale chairs are in keeping with the period. (Moffatt-Ladd House, Portsmouth, N. H., 1763)

63

63. The beautiful hand-painted Chinese paper of this dining room in a Salem, Mass., mansion (1782) is set off by the simple white woodwork, 18th-century chairs and late Sheraton sideboard.

64

64. The dining room of the John Brown House in Providence, Rhode Island (1787), has architectural doorways, dado and cornice, well set off by a scenic paper small enough in scale not to detract from their rather extraordinary grandeur.

65. In a Federal house grey and white paint, in contrasting tones, brings out the architectural features of this late 18th-century paneling. An immense convex mirror, flanked by a pair of old portraits, almost overpowers a Sheraton sideboard. But the symmetry of the entire wall saves the day. An immensely long folding table is surrounded by chairs with the curving lines of the period. (Harrison Grey Otis House, Boston, Mass., 1795)

66. In the simple dining room of the Adams Mansion, Quincy, Mass., stands a Hepplewhite sideboard with crystal candelabra, while the knife boxes which usually stand on the sideboard are on a side table at the right. Old portraits and Federal chairs complete the setting and all have historic reasons for being here. This home of presidents was built in 1731, but withstood many changes and alterations.

65

66

67. The state dining room in the Governor Gore Mansion, (1802-04), in Waltham, Mass., contains formal features, such as a marble floor, late 18th-century mantelpiece, tall gilt mirror, and tall-case clock surmounted by two trumpeting angels. The bare simplicity of the tall walls sets off the handsome furniture.

68

68. A smaller, more informal dining room in the same house has lower ceiling, smaller table, chintz curtains and an altogether more intimate family atmosphere. The graceful small sideboard carries a beautiful silver urn and candelabra, while the extreme curves of two Empire chairs against the wall contrast with the straight lines of those at the table. Again note the simplicity of the wall treatment, which always sets off fine furniture to the best advantage. Never be afraid of simplicity where quality is involved.

69.

69. Late classic pilasters and decoration are combined with a simple mirror, marble mantel, crystal chandelier and candlesticks to good advantage in this formal, Salem dining room. (circa 1818)

70

Bedrooms

70. This early interior of the 17th century shows the primitive construction. The most striking and adaptable idea in the room is the captivating and decorative arrangement of two little wall cupboards separated by open shelves, leveling the sloped-back chimney front above the fireplace. Old pine and rough plaster walls are completely ideal as a background for brightly colored chintz or printed linen, as in the quilted coverlet of the low-post bed. (Old Ironworks House, Saugus, Mass., before 1640)

71

71. A ground floor bedroom was customary in the early days. One in an old Massachusetts farmhouse here receives charming treatment in the richly colored bed curtains of original old material, a gaily patterned quilt, hooked rugs, hanging shelves and old stretcher table filled with brown and yellow earthenware. The natural tone of age in old pine boards is a deep grey-tan, and artistically "right" with the rich reds, browns, greens and blues of old materials.

72

73

72. A bedroom in an old house in Essex, Mass. Slanting rays of sunshine penetrate the simple checked window curtains made in double sets, one on each sash. The old desk-on-frame carries a shelf clock and has a suitably high chair. A lantern hangs from the beam above, and other light is given by the candle in a wrought iron stand on the high chest of drawers, and two in the wooden floor stand with ratchet for adjusting the level. Braided and hooked rugs, a high settle, and an early looking glass are other completely authentic furnishings of this old bedroom. The swinging wooden crane upon which things were hung to dry near the fire may offer a novel use in the contemporary home as a temporary curtain partition for screening one part of a room off from another.

73. Some interesting early beds had a partial canopy, into which the bed folded in the daytime for economy of space in the early houses where an entire family lived in two or three rooms until time and prosperity made it possible to add more. This bed is dressed with a material of old design, a chest stands at its foot, and a Queen Anne lowboy with contemporary looking glass at the right. The beautiful wide floor boards are bare, and the whole unadorned character of the room is authentic and unpretentiously comfortable. (Mission House, Stockbridge, Mass., 1739)

74

75

76

74. An early bed with small canopy is dressed in old cotton material with hand-netted fringe in this bedroom of an old Salem, Mass., house (1651). The note of cool simplicity is carried out by bare floors partially covered with braided mats, and simple cotton window curtains which do not detract from the old inside folding shutters. A Boston rocker stands in the light of the window, and barely visible at the left is a Queen Anne dressing table.

75. A bedroom of utmost simplicity, but considerable comfort, in a Marblehead, Mass. house has off-white plaster walls and wood trim of a soft warm green which might be termed light olive, and which was the original color used here. This was found by careful scraping of the layers of paint and matching of the last one exposed. Curtains are light gold-colored muslin, and the simple modern beds are covered with a copy of an English 18th-century flowered cretonne, with green bindings.

76. Another bedroom in the same house, of spacious and pleasant proportions, contains a Queen Anne highboy, surmounted by a large old luster pitcher. The Sheraton bureau has four reeded posts, the original pine floor boards are slightly darkened and waxed. The walls are natural plaster, the paint a Williamsburg light blue-green, curtains a faded hyacinth or mauve. Other color notes are eggplant, strong blue, and pale rose touches in the old bed coverlet.

77

77. The symmetry of the two windows at the end of this bedroom in the Antiquarian House in Concord, Mass., is accented by a single draped curtain on each, to left and right. This arrangement also lets in more light. The wall unit is centered in the fine block-front chest of drawers above which hangs an early mirror. An old corner cupboard, paneled inside shutters, and a tester bed with ball-and-claw feet and dressed in toile de Jouy, complete the authenticity of this interior.

78. The mantelpiece in this old bedroom of a Salem house is of unusually interesting design, and is faced with original pictorial tiles. A comb-back Windsor rocker stands nearby. The upper section of the fine highboy has probably been shortened by the depth of one drawer in order to fit under the low ceiling. The wallpaper is a copy of a charmingly simple old pattern, a netted bed canopy and hand crocheted coverlet adorn the field bed, and the general keynote is New England simplicity rather than richness or luxury.

79. The dignity of this authentic mid-18th-century bedroom in another Salem, Mass., house is in its finely proportioned paneling, marred only by the placing of a picture over the fireplace in such a way as to deface the lines of the panels. Granted, this is often a problem. Feature either the picture or the paneling alone, but not the two together unless the one fits into the other as in a frame. The netted canopy on the graceful field bed contributes an airy transparency of atmosphere.

78

79

80

81

82

80. The Peirce-Nichols House, Salem, Mass., (1782) contains some of the finest wood-work from the hand of Samuel McIntire, Salem's master builder, architect and wood carver. The wallpaper in this bedroom, though of authentic design, is a little overpower-ingly heavy for the delicacy of the carving. The detail of the mantelpiece, its over-panel and the cornice were added by McIntire after 1800. Two old bonnet stands stare in somewhat startling manner from the serpentine-front chest of drawers. The fine field bed with carved posts is early 19th century, and covered with an original old chintz coverlet. Placing a chest at the foot was logical, convenient and customary.

81. Sarah Orne Jewett's home (c. 1780) in South Berwick, Maine, contains this com-fortable bedroom with finely detailed woodwork, decorative paper of bold and interest-ing design, and a gracefully curved field bed, whose downy depths are approached by means of a diminutive footstool.

82. The Pingree House in Salem (1804) is generally considered Samuel McIntire's masterpiece, and is certainly a gem of the Federal period. These interiors cannot be matched for the completeness, accuracy and beauty of their furnishings. This bedroom has window and bed valances of a lovely French blue embroidered with tiny roses, fur-niture generally Hepplewhite or Sheraton in style, French and American ornaments. The mantelpiece of delicate simplicity is surmounted by a Federal mirror, two Botticelli prints and a pair of French bronze and crystal candle holders, forming a pattern of perfection in taste and arrangement.

83

83. Another bedroom in the Pingree House shows McIntire's wheat sheaves, and other characteristic details in the mantelpiece. Hangings are beautifully made from a pattern of the period. A fine little Sheraton work stand with ivory silk reel stands in the foreground.

84

Post Federal (19th century) Rooms

84. An old mansion in Salem, built in 1822-1823, shows the architectural trend of the Post-Federal period. Empire and Greek Revival influences are evident in cornice moldings and the decorated ceiling, from which hangs a fine crystal chandelier. Its prisms reflect the glitter of the candelabras on the Italian marble mantel whose free-standing Ionic columns and classic Greek floral detail have the character of the period. A Federal convex mirror, shield-back Hepplewhite chairs, and furniture of other periods are harmoniously related in this dignified interior.

85   86

85. The spacious hallway of a Beacon Hill mansion in Boston, built in 1818, shows great enlargement and elaboration of the door lights and leads. Architectural doorways show Greek inspiration in their shaped pediments, the honeysuckle motif and other details used. Great mahogany doors and painted trim set off furniture of the Georgian and Federal periods. An exceptionally handsome example of a city house of the period, now the property of the Women's City Club.

86. Through another doorway in the same house is seen a grey marble mantelpiece in the dining room.

87. A drawing room of the Post-Federal period whose wide expanses are supported by columns, is furnished with family pieces dating from the early Dutch-back chair, through Chippendale, to Empire and Victorian. The windows are curtained with transparent lace, and topped by lambrequins of French blue brocade. Thus did a 19th century home, in Salem, Mass., grow and acquire, along with inherited pieces, a certain amount of clutter, a certain amount of comfort, and the undeniable character of a home.

88. A mantel of white Italian marble is surrounded by an elegant glitter of crystal, gilt, and porcelain, in the Women's City Club, described in No. 85.

87

88

89

90

91   92

89. The pre-revolutionary Vassall-Craigie-Longfellow house in Cambridge, Mass. (1759) contains many furnishings of Longfellow's time (1831-1882). Victorian tasselled hangings curtain the recessed windows in the drawing room.

90. The library at Orchard House, Concord, Mass., home of Louisa May Alcott. No decorator's dream, the room is cluttery but full of personal and living charm because of associations and evidence of use.

91. The drawing room of the Daland Mansion (1849), now the Essex Institute, Salem, Mass., is completely Victorian. The Rogers group and "transparencies" on the table, flowered carpet, large oil paintings and carved furniture are purest evidences of this impure style.

92. Damask curtains in the same room hang from heavy gilded cornices, and a ghostly marble lady gazes from the corner. The note is one of lavish elegance.

93

Odd Rooms

BARS

93. The tap room of the old Buckman Tavern at Lexington, Mass., (1690), catered to the Minute Men of Paul Revere's time but forms a good contemporary design for present day eating and drinking. Of right-angle corner construction, faced with feathered boards, it might mask a complete small kitchen. Candles light the counter and shelves hold ancient jugs and bottles.

94 **95**

94. A miniature tavern bar in the Frary House, Deerfield, Mass. (early 1800's), is entered from the back, or by the horizontally divided door in front. A closet could be transformed to this use by the simple expedient of putting in such a door with a shelf for serving on the lower section, and the necessary storage shelves and equipment within.

95. At Beauport, East Gloucester, Mass., is this serving bar handy to the dining table in the pine kitchen. The half door allows illumination from the window beyond.

96

98

96. This view of the same room shows how such a kitchen-bar could easily be constructed by erecting a simple partition across the end of your dining room, placing the door opening opposite the window, with convenient shelves and cupboards built in on each side.

97. The tap room of the Hall Tavern at Deerfield, Mass. (c. 1760), shows the old wicket which was lowered at closing time over the bar. Not bad as a hint in any day and age.

98. The bar at the Wayside Inn., South Sudbury, Mass., (1686), shows the wicket raised, a welcome to all comers. The counter is mahogany, the front faced with vertical boards, and there is ample working space beyond.

99

PLAY ROOMS

AND ATTICS

99. The old ballroom at Longfellow's Wayside Inn has seen many a gay evening of dancing to the fiddlers, who played in the raised corner area behind the railing. For fiddlers substitute radio and record-player—and use the same corner for storage of folding chairs and games.

100. A room for games and dancing, ping-pong, billiards or music might well use this charming one in an old house in New Haven, Conn., as a model. Candelabras hanging from the vaulted ceiling give good illumination. (Pardee-Morris House, New Haven, Conn., 1680; burnt by the British in 1779, and rebuilt in 1779-80).

101. A more formal ballroom in the Frary House, Deerfield, Mass., which was once a tavern. Large recesses on each side of the chimney could serve as storage space for anything from onlookers to television cabinets. It is worth noting that all of these old ballrooms have built-in benches along the walls, eliminating the need for all those extra chairs at a party.

100

101

102

103

104

102. What to do with sloping attic roofs or gables is shown at Beauport, where a paper of spreading branches and blossoms covers and minimizes awkward planes and angles. The low post bed fits easily under the roof.

103. An ell of the same room shows how furniture, and even a door can be fitted to awkward spaces.

104. Simple wall-board partitions and a little whitewash transform the loft of the Rum Shop in Salem, Mass. (1800), into living quarters. Book-shelves, rugs, comfortable chairs and lamps—and presto a charming informal apartment. **105.** Behind another partition is the small but comfortable bedroom.

106. This picturesque attic of the House of Seven Gables in Salem, Mass. (1668), shows interesting timber construction, and chests conveniently stowed away below the eaves. In this day of modern insulation a really liveable room could be made, keeping some of the same effect.

105

106

107

108

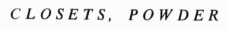
109

CLOSETS, POWDER ROOMS and ODD CORNERS

107. The difficulty of furnishing a small recess or ell of a room is here solved with an old tavern table for writing, an early ladder-back chair with turned posts, and an inviting shelf of books above. (Mission House, Stockbridge, Mass., 1739)

108. An exquisite little Sheraton stand of pale maple fills an awkward spot, a slender accent against dark paneling. (Beauport).

109. Another solution of the odd corner problem. With a good mirror this becomes a charming dressing table recess. The scalloped valance frames and separates it from the rest of the room. (Beauport).

110

111

112

110. An awkward hall or stairway corner may be well adapted for writing. This unusual old desk is lighted by an oval window under the eaves. (Beauport, East Gloucester, Mass.)

111. In this insignificant closet behind the stairs in her simple family home (1790), in Nantucket, Maria Mitchell, famous woman astronomer did most of her writing. If such a great mind could expand in this tiny space, should the rest of us demand more? Perhaps the point was—seclusion, and light.

112. A windowless closet, or powder room, may be charmingly lighted by a blind window of Gothic style, clear panes in front, ground glass in back, through which hidden lights illuminate a collection of amethyst glass on the shelves between.

113

114

Decorative Features

Wall Treatments

113. Stencils were used instead of paper in many old houses and were applied in various combinations of color and pattern.

114. Fanciful stencils decorate a simple plastered chimney in the Hall Tavern (c. 1760), at Deerfield, Mass. The technique of cutting and applying stencils is not difficult to master and offers an inexpensive outlet for that urge to create things for yourself.

115

115. Stencils may be as elaborate or as simple as desired. Often borders alone were used on a tinted plaster wall. (Hall Tavern, Deerfield, Mass. c. 1760)

116

117

118.

116. Some early decorators prided themselves on their freehand painted designs used instead of stencils. This pattern in red, green, and black on a white wall has been restored from clear traces of the original. (Asa Stebbins House, Deerfield, Mass., 1799)

117. A close-up view of the same painted pattern.

118. In a Federal room (1805) in Salem, Mass., this charming wall painting was done by an artist in imitation of the 18th-century style of old papers and ship paintings. It includes the portrayal of a ship actually once in the possession of the family. A very personal touch of this sort might include anything from your great-grandfather's covered wagon to your own yacht. The stenciled Hitchcock chairs, a style not made until after 1820, are quite harmonious with the Queen Anne table and Sheraton sideboard, proving themselves to be one of the most useful pieces of furniture ever designed in this country.

93

119

120

121

122

119. A section of beautiful block-printed scenic paper known as the "Roman Chase" is complete over-mantel decoration in itself in a Federal house in Danversport, Mass. (Samuel Fowler House—1810)

120. In the same house a rare old paper designed in vertical panels covers the walls of the entrance hall, unmarred by superimposed pictures or any additional decoration.

121. A French paper representing the earth's arctic, temperate, and tropical zones decorates an old dining room in Salem, Mass. Sheraton chairs and a sideboard laden with old silver, complete the picture.

122. The individual note appears again at Elmwood, former home of James Russell Lowell in Cambridge, Mass., where an exterior view of the house itself appears on the stairway wall. A photomural might be used in this way.

123

124

Window Treatments

123 & 124. Small-paned windows with heavy muntins and narrow frames which do not extend over the plaster wall surface identify a certain type of early or Mid-Colonial house. Their individual character is accented in Fig. 124, rather than disguised, by completely simple muslin curtains hung by small loops within the window frame itself. The wooden rods drop into open wooden brackets set inside the frame of the window. The same method is used in the living room (Fig. 123) to hang unlined ivory Glosheen curtains, with Williamsburg-blue scalloped borders and tie-backs which match the painted trim.

125

125. Gracefully and simply draped lined damask hangings fall to slightly below mid-window level, leaving the glass uncovered and fold-in shutters unobstructed. An authentic 18th-century design. (Derby House, Salem, Mass., 1760-62)

126   **127**

126. Bright red cotton hangings frame interesting painted window shades in a room at Beauport, East Gloucester, Mass. The walls are deep brown, old curtain tie-backs of brass. An ivory yarn-reel is placed in the center of the table.

127. Other windows in the same room have a single curtain drawn back to one side only, with a heavy tassel opposite. The unusual painted shades, when drawn, are an important decorative feature of the room.

128. Elaborate taffeta hangings of late 18th-century style are an important decorative element in this Federal room. Venetian blinds were used in the 18th century. (Pingree House, Salem, Mass., 1804)

129. Curtains in the Pingree House drawing room are of soft embroidered mull, draped after a pattern of the Federal period, and fringed. They are not difficult to copy for a room inspired by the Federal style. The Chinese Chippendale card table seems to invite a friendly group to this well lighted corner between two windows. The table is surrounded by shield-back Hepplewhite chairs, and two tall candle stands are close at hand to light an evening game.

128

129

130

131

132

130. The use of a door for a window, and even as window becoming a cabinet for old glass, sounds the essence of incongruity until seen in the hall at Beauport, where amber and brown glass in all shapes and sizes glints against the light. The same idea in simplified form may be used with any window if you are willing to sacrifice air for decoration. Use leaded panes and fanlight for the inner section for a decorative feature of extraordinary interest.

131. Formally draped hangings make a single unit of a group of windows in a bay, consistent with the dignified architectural style of this dining room, in a Salem, Mass., mansion.

Beds

132. An early type of tester bed is dressed in embroidered curtains of the period. At its foot stands a Connecticut chest with applied split spindle decoration. (Mission House, Stockbridge, Mass., 1739)

133

134

133. This Hepplewhite bed is dressed in gay flowered chintz which contrasts with the plain material of the skirted coverlet. The canopy is lined with the plain material decoratively gathered to a central rosette. (Beauport.)

134. Simplicity itself is this graceful maple field bed with transparent netted canopy in an old Deerfield, Mass., house.

135. A more elaborate netted canopy hangs low over the posts of this field bed without hiding their graceful contours, in a bedroom of an ancient house in Ipswich, Mass.

135

136

136. Another example of the decoratively lined chintz canopy, in a Salem, Mass., mansion.

137. The tester of this bed forms an exposed cornice simply trimmed with a gathered valance. The coverlet is an old quilted one of printed chintz—rose and blue on a deep eggplant background.

138. A high-post bed with decorative tester cornice is handsomely dressed in blue and apricot damask in a Federal bedroom. (Pingree House, Salem, Mass., 1804.)

137   **138**

139

Decorative Groups and Details

139. A most unusual early 18th-century portable desk has the single brass drop pulls of the William and Mary period. A pair of brass candlesticks of early type, and the early 18th-century "courting mirror" complete this simple group. (Derby House, Salem, Mass., 1761.)

140

141

140. A rather uncompromisingly stiff old pine settle fills a useful as well as decorative purpose in a hallway. A group of quaint early prints are placed in a row above it, consistently following the straight lines of the furniture and wall. The chair at the left is of the Carver type with heavy posts and spindles in the back.

141. A tiny but well lighted dressing room in the Lee Mansion, Marblehead, Mass. (1768), contains a dressing table simply decorated with authentic old printed cotton of small and charming pattern. On it stands an ivory trinket box. The mirror is American Chippendale, suitably flanked by a pair of brass candle brackets. The Queen Anne highboy has brasses of the period and carries an old bandbox covered with wallpaper. The latter offers a good idea for the home craftsman.

142

143

144

145

146

142. A Windsor armchair is comfortable before a Sheraton wall table used as a simple desk. The American Chippendale mirror and a pair of gilded brackets holding decorative carvings complete a harmoniously arranged group.

143. A fretted and gilt Chippendale mirror complements a Queen Anne dressing table.

144. A Sheraton sideboard over a large Chinese porcelain jar carries a pair of fine old knife boxes, a painted tray, and delicate and graceful silver. A well composed group.

145. Group small pictures into a pattern rather than dissipate their effect by scattering them.

146. A superb example of the Federal Girandole mirror. (A mirror with candle brackets.)

147

148

149

150

147. A detail of a McIntire fireplace in the Pingree House shows his wheat sheaf and other characteristic details. The Lowestoft urn is a deep orange-yellow.

148. A Victorian grouping of gilt and enameled clock with ruby glass decanters upon an incongruous Gothic shelf has an inexplicable but undeniable charm. Even the confused pattern of the wallpaper background contributes to, rather than detracts, from the effect.

149. Crystal candelabra at Gore Place.

150. The fragile beauty of a late 18th-century candelabra on a Sheraton flap-top card table is composed of marble, porcelain, brass and crystal.

Cupboards

and

Shelves

151

151. A book might be written about cupboards and shelves. Nothing in the house so completely combines the purposes of utility and decoration. Nothing offers such a wide variety of style and purpose as cupboards, secretaries, and dressers. Nothing has been more constantly in use through the centuries than shelves—built-in or portable. Here is a basically simple example of shelves constructed in varying spaces to accommodate pewter chargers and plates, wide and small. The unchanged background wall of feathered pine sheathing stretches from ceiling beam to exposed sill.

152

153

154

152. The most primitive style of wooden dresser, with correct old wooden knob pulls on drawers and doors, may be built-in or portable. Pewter chargers, wooden plates, mugs and jugs and pots are its burden. A small bracket shelf holds spice boxes, mortar and pestle. Horizontal feathered sheathing shows this to be an outside wall of the house. (John Ward House, Salem, Mass., 1684)

153. In your pine paneled dining room or kitchen build in an open dresser with scroll cut ends to hold the more decorative china. The doors of the lower section of this one are of feathered boards, with several drawers in the center pulled by the correct early small wooden knobs. The slope front cupboard on the right is also an old charmer. (Beauport, East Gloucester, Mass.)

154. A homely and simple old dresser which practically spells "utility" is simply and reasonably housed between two projecting wall cupboards, leveling a wall surface and leaving no bruising corners. Scroll cut cornice top and sides, open shelves above, an interestingly varied lower space combining drawers, closed cupboard with beveled panel door, and open section. (Tristram Coffin House, Newbury, Mass., c. 1651).

155

156

155. A humble built-in kitchen dresser is made decorative with old platters, jugs and pots. Drawers below and built in against the wall at the right.

156. How to use a corner for cupboard space is shown in an easy-to-copy two-sided dresser with scroll-trimmed top and sides. Flat lower section completely without projections has "H" hinges and wooden catches on the door.

112

157

158

159

157. These shelves with scroll-cut frame are built of old pine across an awkward corner, otherwise hard to reach over the kitchen counter. Three small rounded shelves fill the angle at the right. The space beneath is put to use for hanging saucepans.

158. Walls of the buttery in an old house in Deerfield, Mass., are sheathed with pine boards, joined by a simple beading. Shelves of utmost simplicity hold milk buckets and other utensils.

159. Another easy-to-copy open dresser has shelves of different depths holding a collection of pewter. The overflow is informally accommodated on an extra built-in shelf above.

113

160

161

160. The charm of an unbalanced, informal arrangement is shown in open and closed cupboards set into the pine sheathing above this large fireplace. Ovens at the right might nowadays hold firewood and kindling.

161. A collection of Spode and other old china fills a corner cupboard with interestingly shaped shelves.

162

163

164

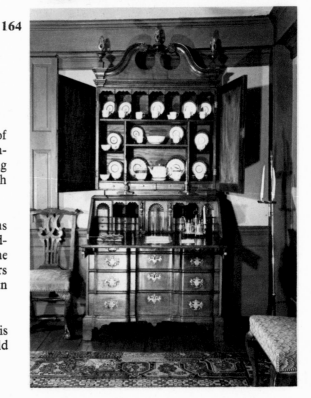

162. A nicely unbalanced arrangement of fireplace and china cupboard for the informal small house is shown in this dining room on Cape Cod. A wide brick hearth extends the length of the wall.

163. A fine built-in corner cupboard forms an important decorative feature of a Mid-Colonial house in Essex, Massachusetts. The arch-top, with shell-carved vault, pilasters and moldings show the early Georgian feeling.

164. An impressive block-front secretary is a distinguished background for fine old china.

115

165

166

167

165. Charming arrangement in a rounded cupboard with curved shelves.

166. A small cupboard in a plain sheathed wall makes a charming overmantel decoration when left open for display of old china.

167. Fine glass and colorful Canton sparkle against a dark background. (Ropes Mansion, Salem, Mass., c. 1719)

116

168

Fireplaces

168. The importance of the great central chimney in the Early American house is shown in this massive fireplace. Heavy oak lintel and wide brick hearth, oven door and huge iron pot, all bespeak utility and warmth. Upon the hearth stand two roasting ovens, a trivet and iron spider. High and dry above hang a musket and powder horn as was customary in the early days. The brick arch supports the second floor hearth and at the same time contributes unconscious style and beauty to the whole. (Stephen Daniel House, Salem, Mass.)

169

170

171

169. This chimney and hearth are made of stone instead of brick. Lintel and walls are covered with fine wide pine sheathing. Furniture, tin candle sconces, pipe box, spit-jack and other cooking implements are all original old pieces. The fireplace shelters a chair within its wide embrace for Granny to keep warm by the fire.

170. The very personification of home and informal comfort, this wide brick hearth carries a Windsor armchair on the right and a quaint double rocking-chair at the left. The small recess built into the paneling above the chimney opening contains graduated pewter measures.

171. This photograph illustrates shadow molding, a method of trimming the seams of pine sheathing with a simple grooved decoration. Here also is the dentil molding, or notched strip which joins sheathing to ceiling beams, and which outlines the fireplace. In old natural pine, with touches of vermilion red in the dentil molding, this Early American fireplace end bears an interesting resemblance to modern designs in its simplicity of style. (Hart House, Ipswich, Mass., 1640)

172

172. A simple old fireplace surrounded by feathered boards, remarkable for their size as are the great beams above. Again we see a curiously modern feeling in this flat undecorated Early American wall.

173. A slightly recessed fireplace is here surrounded by feathered sheathing, each board having one beveled edge which is set into a groove in the next. Dentil molding trims the fireplace opening. Upon the hearth stands a tiny old pine bench sometimes called a "cricket."

174. A fireplace in this Early American house has been surrounded by rectangular panels, boxed-in beams and plastered ceiling of the Mid-Colonial period (Stephen Daniel House, Salem, Mass.)

173

174

175

176

177

175. Another charming bedroom fireplace, is placed in a recess just deep enough to cast a shadow and hold a narrow useful shelf. The opening is decorated with old tiles.

176. A simple Mid-Colonial dining room shows a fireplace end of charmingly unsymmetrical design. Windsor chairs and old pewter complete the picture.

177. The slightly recessed fireplace with simple, strongly beveled panels adds great interest to the design of this bedroom wall.

178

179

180

181

178. Restrained good taste in a perfect arrangement about a small fireplace. The old beams, exposed above, the stiff settle with protecting curtain hanging behind it, show the very early period of this house. But again we see the curiously modern feeling of the simple fireplace and wall.

179. This more formal Mid-Colonial fireplace shows a distinctly Georgian character in fluted pilasters, bolection molding around the fireplace, and raised panel above. (Mission House, Stockbridge, Mass., 1739)

180. Ingenuity and imagination are shown in the arrangement and varying sizes of these panels. Typical of the Mid-Colonial period, they are still quite at home with earlier furniture and implements.

181. The simplicity of a Quaker home in Nantucket, Mass., is shown in the kitchen of the Maria Mitchell House (1790). A Boston rocker stands at left. The woodwork is painted to imitate the grain of natural wood. This was fairly common in 18th-century decoration.

182

183

184

182. A bedroom fireplace in the Lee Mansion, Marblehead, Mass. (1768), is charmingly simple in design, faced with decorative tiles and slightly recessed within the wall.

183. The high ceiling, complicated cornice, Corinthian pilasters and carved mantel of this room typify the Georgian-Colonial style which came to its peak in the third quarter of the 18th century. The chair at the right is a Queen Anne roundabout, or corner chair. (Wentworth-Gardner House, Portsmouth, N. H., 1760)

184. This exceptionally handsome carved mantelpiece in the Lee Mansion is reminiscent of Grinling Gibbons, the English woodcarver.

185

186

187

185. A bolection molding framing the fire-place, raised panels and Corinthian pilasters are here combined with formal and gracious effect. (Lee Mansion, Marblehead, Mass., 1768)

186. A fireplace-end in the earlier style of Samuel McIntire, woodcarver-architect of Salem, Mass.

187. A simple Federal fireplace is hand-somely decorated with a balanced arrangement of crystal candelabras and old glass decanters. White wallpaper with a motif of gold leaves is harmonious in tone and scale.

189

188. One of Samuel McIntire's finest Federal mantelpieces is this one in the Pingree House, Salem, Mass. (1804). The remarkable old French wallpaper was designed by Fragonard, strong blue classic patterns and border on a golden ground. One of the vertical panels forms a perfect overmantel picture, a useful idea easily adapted in a contemporary setting. A uniquely handsome pair of orange-yellow Lowestoft urns forms the only other decoration. At the left stands an unusual mahogany combined pole screen and candle stand.

189. Handsome details accent this fireplace end designed by Samuel McIntire. An early type of coal-burning grate ornaments the fireplace. The cupboard shelves are filled with Canton china. (Peirce-Nichols House, Salem, Mass., 1782)

190

190. The delicate Federal designs gave way to Empire and Greek Revival styles. Here a marble mantel shows Greek detail of coarse proportions. The decorative arrangement shows how a pair of pictures (in this case very beautiful pastels by John Singleton Copley) may be used in place of the more usual one alone. A French Empire clock centers the composition, completed by pairs of lamps and jars in appropriate scale.